EXPLORING
SEA MYSTERIES

By Anthony Wall

Illustrated by Harry Bishop
and Michael Atkinson

Edited by Jill Coleman

*G*host ships and sea monsters, fabulous riches and strange disappearances; these are some of the mysteries of the deep. A few have been solved, but the sea guards its secrets closely and many strange tales remain unexplained. One such story concerns the sealing ship *Baychimo*. Trapped by ice off Alaska, the ship looked in danger of being ground to pieces. So the crew made camp on a nearby beach. They huddled in their tents for a week while a storm raged outside. When the storm passed, *Baychimo* had gone. The next year, 1932, gold prospectors sighted her drifting 1000 miles east of where she had been trapped. They boarded her, but left when they could not start the engines. In 1933, Eskimo hunters found *Baychimo* over 1000 miles west of her last reported position. They began looting her cargo of sealskins, but were forced to flee when a blizzard sprang up. Since then, *Baychimo* has been seen many times but never "captured". The last sighting was in 1956. Could she still be sailing the Arctic seas with no captain or crew?

Drowned Giant

On April 10, 1912, the British luxury liner *Titanic* set out on her maiden voyage from Southampton to New York. Nearly 1000 feet long with 11 decks, she was the biggest ship ever built and carried over 2,000 people. Everyone knew *Titanic* was the finest ship of all time. Her captain thought her unsinkable. Yet, incredibly, within a week she lay deep beneath the Atlantic Ocean.

Shortly before midnight on April 14, *Titanic* struck an iceberg 95 miles south of Newfoundland. It ripped a 300-foot gash in her side. Less than three hours later, the huge liner sank with the loss of some 1,500 lives.

The tragedy made world news. But some strange circumstances were never explained. *Titanic* had been steaming much too fast (22 knots), although the captain had been warned of ice by radio. There were lifeboats for barely half the people aboard, perhaps because the captain thought his ship unsinkable. Although the liner *Californian* was only 10 miles away, her radio was switched off and she did not recognize *Titanic*'s distress rockets. So it was a more distant liner, *Carpathia*, which finally arrived to save the 711 survivors.

Strangely, the *Titanic* disaster was "predicted" in 1898. An American writer, Morgan Robertson, wrote a story about an imaginary vessel, *Titan*, whose fate was almost the same as *Titanic*'s. Equally strange, one inky night in 1935, the lookout of a ship called *Titanian* realized that he was sailing towards the very spot where *Titanic* had sunk on the date he was born. He called the alarm and *Titanian* stopped. An iceberg towered ahead!

Coincidence, or mysteriously linked?

Monsters and Mermaids

A huge and horrible head on a long, thick neck reared out of the water. Two fierce yellow eyes glared at the man in the boat. Not surprisingly, he rowed for his life.

It was a sunny June day in 1808. A clergyman called Maclain and 13 other boat-owners had gone fishing off the west coast of Scotland. But none of them wanted to catch a sea monster! Terrified, they all raced towards the shore. Later, everyone agreed that the creature which had chased them was between 70 and 80 feet long, with a brown body.

Did Maclain and his friends only imagine the monster? If so, could hundreds of people who saw one like it in August, 1817, also have been mistaken? For 13 days, an enormous sea serpent was watched by crowds from the port of Gloucester, Massachusetts, USA. It lazed on the water, played, or caught shoals of herrings. Members of the Boston Society of Naturalists who came to investigate saw the serpent from less than 150 yards away. It was over 90 feet long, swimming in a series of humps at about 30 mph.

In spite of many reports like these, most biologists insist that prehistoric sea monsters do not exist. Often "sea serpents" have turned out to be giant squids, lines of swimming turtles, or even porpoises following each other.

But monsters have been recorded for centuries. In 1848, the British warship *Daedalus* came close to a serpent in the Atlantic. Those aboard studied the huge beast for 20 minutes. It was over 70 feet long and had a mane. A serpent almost as big as this was spotted by a British submarine captain. He and his crew saw the beast on the surface of the water and fired at it from less than 90 feet away.

If monsters exist, do mermaids? Half fish, half human, they are said to have beautiful faces and sweet singing voices which lure sailors beneath the waves. Only by marrying a man can a mermaid gain a soul. Legends of mermaids are very old, and some people still claim to have seen them. But scientists suggest that mermaids are probably sea mammals such as the dugong and the manatee. These seal-like animals rise out of the water to suckle their young. Could they be mistaken for mermaids, or is there a more mysterious explanation?

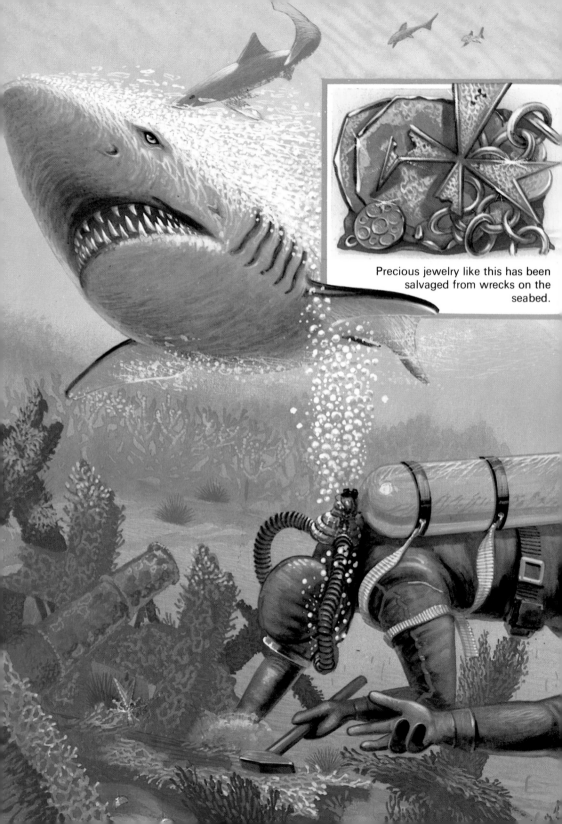

Precious jewelry like this has been salvaged from wrecks on the seabed.

Sunken Treasure

Somewhere on the seabed lies a huge fortune of gold, silver, and precious jewels. Sheltered by the skeletons of ancient ships, at least $500 million worth of treasure lies scattered among the bones of the men who sank with their valuable cargo. Adventurers and scholars have scoured the seabed, attracted by the promise of such fabulous wealth. But treasure hunting is a difficult and sometimes dangerous business.

In the 1960s, Kip Wagner, an American, located the wrecks of a Spanish fleet which sank in a hurricane off Florida on July 31, 1715. When divers began to explore the 11 wrecks, they were surrounded by dozens of interested spectators – great white sharks. These terrible man-eaters, which can grow up to 40 feet long, had never been seen in such numbers. Why so many here? Perhaps they remembered the feast their ancestors had had in 1715. More than 1,000 men died when the ships went down, and some scientists believe that the taste for human flesh may be passed on from one generation of sharks to the next.

Beset by dangers, Wagner and his team found nothing for six months. They were beginning to lose hope when one man surfaced, clutching six wedges of silver. This was the beginning of a series of extraordinary finds. On one occasion, they cleared a layer of sand from the seabed to find a carpet of gold which spread as far as the eye could see. In all, they salvaged a record $7,000,000 of gold, silver, coins and jewels.

Other divers have not been so lucky. A particularly sinister wreck is that of *Santa Maria* in which Columbus sailed to discover America. On a calm Christmas Eve in 1492, the little ship hit a reef near Haiti and later sank.

Nobody has yet been able to salvage *Santa Maria*. Three attempts, in 1954, 1960 and 1972, failed because of freak accidents, including the sudden death of a diver. Will this historic vessel ever be recovered? Or is she cursed by bad luck, as some salvage men think?

Joshua Slocum's boat, *Spray*.

Bermuda

Florida

Puerto Rico

Gone Missing

Ships are not the only things to disappear in the Triangle. In 1945, five TBM bombers flew off course and sank in the Atlantic, another case of navigational instruments mysteriously going wrong.

The huge flying-boat, sent to find the missing bombers, exploded in mid-air about 20 minutes after take off.

The C-119 Flying Boxcar also disappeared in the Triangle. This was later attributed to engine failure.

Commercial airliners have been claimed by the Triangle. The disappearance of the *Star Tiger* in 1948 is still a mystery.

Cyclops

Hundreds of ships are lost at sea every year. Storms and accidents take a heavy toll. But sometimes vessels vanish mysteriously without trace, and rescuers search in vain for wreckage or survivors.

On December 30, 1976, the huge tanker, *Grand Zenith* reported bad weather in the Atlantic. Soon afterwards she lost radio contact. Search vessels were sent out almost immediately, for she was carrying nearly 2 million gallons of oil. But although dozens of ships and aircraft combed several thousand square miles, only elusive traces of her were found. One vessel found a huge oil slick near *Grand Zenith's* last reported position. When a second ship arrived to take samples of the oil, the slick had mysteriously disappeared. On January 19, 1977, the US Coastguard abandoned the search.

Maritime experts are particularly puzzled by the Bermuda Triangle. This notorious stretch of water between Bermuda, Florida and Puerto Rico has been the scene of strange disappearances for centuries.

It has claimed ships of all sorts and sizes. Captain Joshua Slocum and his boat *Spray* weathered a round-the-world trip in the 1890s. But they were never heard of again after sailing into the Bermuda Triangle in 1909. Nine years later, the US navy supply ship *Cyclops* and her crew of 309 men also became victims of the Triangle. The 500-foot vessel silently vanished, although carrying the latest radio equipment.

Modern-day captains returning safely from the Triangle tell weird tales of ships' instruments that "went mad" or of vessels which stopped dead in fog patches and then moved backwards. Joe Talley nearly drowned when his fishing boat *Wild Goose* was suddenly sucked under water. She was being towed by the powerful *Caicos Trader* whose captain cut the tow rope lest his ship be dragged down too.

Ships are still disappearing in the Bermuda Triangle, often on calm, clear days when they are near land. Strange lights in the sky, freak weather conditions and other inexplicable phenomena have been reported.

A whole range of explanations, from flying saucers to bad weather, have been given for these strange happenings. But the mystery has not yet been solved, and many seamen fear to enter this eerie stretch of water.

Abandoned Ships

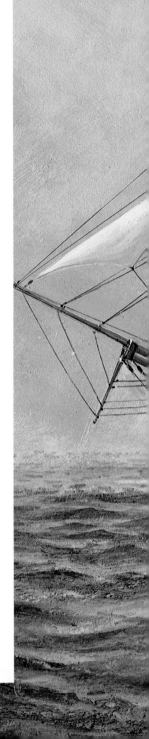

The tale of the *Mary Celeste* is the most famous of all sea mysteries. On December 5, 1872, 600 miles west of Gibraltar, the brigantine *Dei Gratia* came across another ship which seemed to be sailing without the aid of a crew. *Dei Gratia*'s master, Captain Morehouse, sent a three-man boarding party to investigate.

Once aboard the *Mary Celeste*, the sailors began to explore. They found no one. Although slightly battered by the weather, the ship was seaworthy. Everything had been left just as if the crew were still on board. The cargo, barrels of alcohol, was secure in the hold. There was plenty of food and water. The cabins contained the crew's personal possessions, their oilskins and boots, even pipes and tobacco. Only the lifeboat, some navigational instruments and the ship's papers were missing.

Why did the crew abandon the *Mary Celeste* without taking even the basic necessities for survival? After more than 100 years, the answer is still a mystery. The most likely explanation is that Captain Briggs feared an explosion from alcohol fumes leaking from the hold. In panic, he ordered his wife, baby daughter and the seven crew into the lifeboat, with a tow attached to the ship. But a storm blew up, the tow rope snapped, and the ten were left to the merciless sea.

This was not the last of the mishaps to befall the *Mary Celeste*. She met with several other "accidents" before she ended her days. Some say that her last captain deliberately wrecked her on a reef near Haiti.

Nobody can be sure what happened, but one thing is known. The owner of the *Mary Celeste* had broken a legendary rule of the sea – he had changed her name.

There are even stranger cases than the *Mary Celeste* mystery. In 1881, the schooner *Ellen Austin* met an empty schooner in the Atlantic. Men from *Ellen Austin* boarded the abandoned ship to take her as a prize. Then a storm separated the vessels. When they made contact again, the boarding crew had disappeared. The lure of a big reward drew a second crew on to the schooner. Soon she was sailing further and further ahead of *Ellen Austin*. The speeding schooner vanished over the horizon for ever!

Phantoms Afloat

The captain of the coaster *Edenbridge* gasped. A schooner was sailing straight for his ship. Collision seemed certain. He yelled at the helmsman to change course and, miraculously, the two vessels just missed each other.

That day, February 13, 1798, the captain of another ship in the area saw the same schooner run aground on the notorious Goodwin Sands, off England's southeast coast. But the ship he saw did not really exist. Exactly 50 years earlier, an identical vessel called *Lady Lovibond* had struck the Goodwin Sands and sunk with all aboard. Had the captains sighted her ghost? In 1848, the Deal lifeboat went to help a schooner grounded on the Goodwin Sands. But when the boat arrived, there was no sign of a wreck. The phantom schooner showed up again 50 years later, in 1898, and then in 1948. Will her next appearance be on February 13, 1998?

Some sailors say they have met phantom people at sea. Captain Joshua Slocum, the first man to sail single-handed around the world, claimed he had a ghost for company during most of the three-year trip in his tiny craft *Spray*. The spectre told Slocum he was the pilot of *Pinta*, one of Columbus's ships, and would guide *Spray* through danger. According to Slocum, the pilot saved *Spray* several times before she returned safely to America.

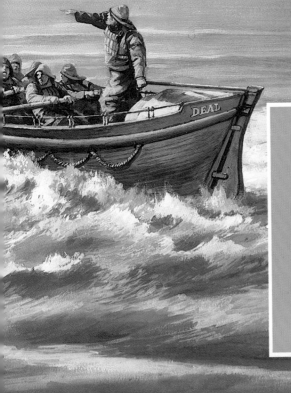

The most famous haunted ship of all time was the *Great Eastern*. So many disasters befell her that she came to be known as a jinxed ship. Passengers used to complain of strange knockings coming from the bowels of the ship. Their tales were dismissed as superstitious nonsense. But when the ship was scrapped in 1888, workmen found the skeletons of two riveters who had been sealed up inside her while she was being built!

What Went Wrong?

The paddle-driven *Birkenhead* was the British navy's first iron steamer. In the early morning of February 26, 1852, while carrying troops and some of their families to South Africa, she struck a rock near the Cape of Good Hope. *Birkenhead* sank with the loss of 445 lives. Whinnying horses leapt over the ship's side and swam for the shore. But none reached land. Sharks tore them to pieces.

The women and children on board were rowed to safety in the only three serviceable boats. The rest of the vessel's complement, more than 550 soldiers and sailors, stayed on board to await their fate. They stood in rows, proud and erect, while a piper played. Soon *Birkenhead* broke up and was swallowed by the sea. Some men were later saved, including 40 who clung to a mast. But most died, as bravely as they would have done in battle.

Birkenhead was way off course when she hit the rock. Why? How could so experienced a captain as Master Com-

mander Salmond make such a blunder? The probable answer is that he did not but his compass did. The iron of the ship may have made the compass give a false reading, or perhaps it was affected by electricity in the atmosphere. That would explain the sad *Birkenhead* mystery.

But how can we explain another accident, on 22 June, 1893, when two British battleships collided off Tripoli, Syria. Admiral Tryon, a great naval strategist, was conducting maneuvers of 15 steam warships. Suddenly, he gave an order which was bound to result in his flagship *Victoria* being rammed by her sister ship *Camperdown*. Tryon was among the 358 men who died when *Victoria* sank.

What went wrong? Just before the accident, the Admiral was "seen" at his wife's tea party in London. Did Tryon's "ghost" give the order on *Victoria*? Or was the ship doomed after her name was changed – from *Renown* – as the sailors' superstition goes?

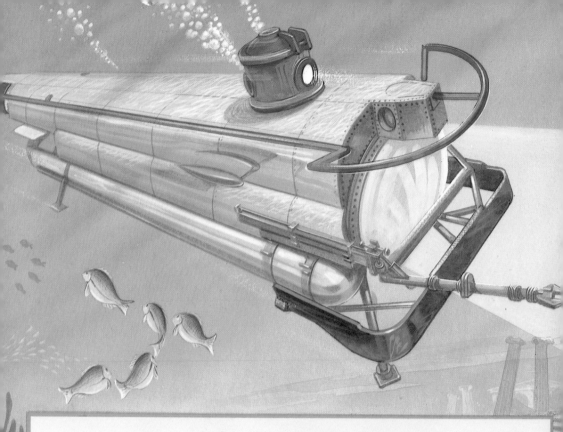

The City Beneath the Sea

Once there was a beautiful land, bigger than Africa and Asia put together, whose inhabitants had everything that the heart could desire. They were healthy, good-looking, rich, clever and contented. The city-dwellers lived in houses of red and black stone with golden roofs, and country people farmed the fertile soil of lush valleys. The mountains were full of minerals and the rivers full of fish. This paradise was powerful, too, mustering mighty armies to conquer other lands.

Then disaster struck. In a single day, 11,500 years ago, the whole continent sank beneath the Atlantic Ocean. So goes the legend of Atlantis. Plato, the great Greek philosopher, told this story 9,000 years later. Since then, man has dreamed of finding the lost continent. Did Atlantis exist? No one can yet answer that. But there are some interesting possibilities. For example, small islands would become huge if the Atlantic Ocean were to subside only 600 feet.

Was the earth suddenly drowned by a flood? Legends of such a disaster are common to all races. Science shows that land and sea levels have altered dramatically through the ages. The Sahara desert was once water and the Mediterranean Sea land. Fish fossils have even been found in mountains.

According to Plato, Atlantis was an Atlantic continent. But many people now believe it was merely a city and situated elsewhere. Ruins, some 10,000 to 12,000 years old, have been found in the Caribbean Sea. Were these Atlantis? Or was the city, as some believe, on the Greek island of Thera in the Mediterranean? Around 1,500 BC, Thera was the scene of history's biggest-ever volcanic eruption. It blew a hole in the center of the island, causing massive tidal waves which would have flooded any land in their path. Is Atlantis lying at the bottom of the hole, under water? Excavations of Thera's historic sites suggest this is possible. But for now, at least, the Atlantis mystery remains.

The *Antelope*, a 300-ton ship belonging to the East India Company, as she looked when she set out from Macao.

Shape-Changer

With a fair wind filling her sails, *Antelope* was as graceful a ship as ever put to sea. She left the Chinese port of Macao one spring day in 1783 and headed home to Britain. Months passed and no word came from *Antelope*. She must have sunk or been seized by pirates, her owners gloomily decided.

Then, just before Christmas, a curious incident occurred. A sailor on the Macao waterfront noticed a ship approaching. At first, he wanted to laugh, she was the funniest looking vessel he had ever seen. Yet, somehow he felt he knew her. When the ship moored at the wharf he read her name, *Antelope*. What had happened? How had the trim little vessel turned into such an odd and ugly shape?

Her crew told an astonishing tale. Six weeks after leaving Macao, *Antelope* ran aground on a reef. The crew, taking supplies and guns, rowed to a nearby island. It turned out to be uninhabited, with plenty of fresh water. Soon, two canoes appeared from a neighboring island. *Antelope's* men prepared to repel hostile natives. But the intruders only wanted guns and help to fight a neighboring tribe. So the sailors helped them to beat their enemies.

Meanwhile, the rest of the crew began rebuilding *Antelope* from the wreck of the first vessel. At last, in November, she set sail, reaching Macao for Christmas. So the mystery of the ship that changed shape was solved.

Fact or Fiction

The superstitions of the sea are endless. Lord Nelson, Britain's great naval hero, attached a horseshoe to the mainmast of his flagship *Victory* for luck. Many mariners would not whistle at sea for fear of causing a gale. Even today, a yachtsman may put a coin under the mast of his boat to ensure good fortune.

Ill-fated Figureheads Sailors used to think that the spirit of a ship lived in its figurehead and protected the crew from danger. But some figureheads were considered unlucky. In 1861, the sailing ship *Maritana* was wrecked. Most of the crew were killed, but the figurehead was unharmed. This was the third ship to sink bearing the same figurehead.

Unlucky Launch It is still believed to be bad luck to change a ship's name, and worse still for something to go wrong at her launching. Both happened to *Great Eastern* whose 30-year career was dogged by disaster. The first attempt to launch *Leviathan*, as she was then known, killed 3 workers and injured 12. At the second attempt, more than 100 spectators were hurt when a viewing stand collapsed. The third attempt, on January 31, 1858, was successful. But on that day, the owners of *Leviathan* went bankrupt. She was sold to another company and re-named *Great Eastern*. Worse trouble loomed and she eventually became known as a haunted ship.

The Flying Dutchman This old seafaring yarn tells of a ghostly ship that must sail the Cape of Good Hope for ever because her captain, Van Derdeken, gambled with the devil and lost his soul. Bad luck is supposed to come to all who see the ghost ship. Some claim they have seen her. But it seems unlikely, since the *Flying Dutchman* and her mad captain were invented by a French writer 300 years ago.

A Magic Island The legendary island of Hy Brazil is said to appear in the sunset to those who are holy enough to see it. On its heights is a glass castle full of people.

At the prow of a ship was the figurehead, said to hold the spirit of the ship.

The magical glass castle on the island of Hy Brazil, off the Irish coast.

Index

This edition produced for K mart Corporation, Troy, Michigan
© Piper Books Ltd. 1980
All rights reserved
Printed by Worzalla Publishing Co., Stevens Point, Wisconsin